PORTUGAL

A PICTURE BOOK TO REMEMBER HER BY

Designed by
DAVID GIBBON

Produced by
TED SMART

CRESCENT

INTRODUCTION

Occupying the western part of the Iberian Peninsula, Portugal's narrow strip of land is flanked by the mighty Atlantic Ocean and isolated from the rest of Europe by the rugged bulk of Spain.

One of Europe's oldest countries, her earliest history is evidenced in Paleolithic and Neolithic discoveries, with Iron Age cultures predominant in the north by 500 BC. The blood of these early, dark-skinned and thick-set Iberians, who were the primary racial strain in a scattered population, would, as the result of invasion and trade, become mixed with those of the Celts, Phoenicians, Moors and Jews.

Portugal derives her name from Portus Cale, a pre-Roman or Roman settlement, near the mouth of the Douro River. When the Romans arrived, in the 3rd century BC, attracted by its wealth of olive oil and wine, they were met with resistance from the Lusitani, a Celtic federation led by Viriathus, a brilliant chieftain from the hills, who kept the Romans at bay until his assassination enabled Decius Junius Brutus to march through central Portugal and subdue the Gallaeci.

Although the Roman role in Portugal was one of exploitation rather than development, they nevertheless left as a legacy a number of fine, straight roads, aqueducts and bridges, and among the more notable remains are the beautiful Temple of Diana at Évora and the ruins of Conimbriga, one of the richest and most civilised cities of the Luso-Roman epoch.

With the collapse of the Rhine frontier came the invasion of the Barbarians, followed by those of the Goths and Visigoths, and then the Moors, who succeeded in defeating Rodrigo, the last king of the Goths, in 711.

Under Moorish influence orchards of almonds, figs and apricots flourished and irrigation systems introduced that are still being used in the country today. Cities sprang up and prospered and the tolerant Moors offered protection to Christian monks and a welcome to Jews, as a Moorish-Arabian culture spread outward from Coimbra and Kelb.

Throughout the Middle Ages Christian Crusades were undertaken not only to recover the Holy Land from the Moslems, but to oust the Moors from Spain and Portugal. In the 12th century Christian counts and barons from Galicia, Asturias and Léon patiently waited for an opportunity to repel the Infidel and it was during this period that the famous El Cid captured Valencia. One of his comrades-in-arms was a Count of Burgundy who had married Teresa, one of the daughters of the King of Léon, and together they ruled over Portucale, the land located between the Douro and Minho Rivers. It was their son, Afonso Henriques who was to carve out his kingdom by bravely pushing the Moors south, and finally, with tremendous courage, succeeded in capturing seven of the Moorish strongholds, including Lisbon. Afonso's descendants brought order to their kingdom: the poet king Dom Dinis built the first Portuguese fleet and founded the University of Coimbra.

The last of the Burgundian line died, leaving no male heir, and as a result the King of Castile marched on Lisbon to lay claim to the throne. Opponents of Castile chose John, master of Aviz and the illegitimate son of Pedro I, as their leader and declared him defender of the realm. Anxious to preserve their independence the Portuguese rallied to his cause and routed the Castilians at the mighty Battle of Aljubarrota, on the 14th August, 1385. In 1387 John of Aviz married Philippa of Lancaster, the daughter of John of Gaunt and in so doing cemented the Portuguese pact with England, the oldest continuous alliance in Europe.

Of their six children, the most famous was Henry the Navigator. Under his patronage Portuguese seamen explored and colonised Madeira and the Azores, and sailed down the African coast almost to Sierra Leone. His painstaking and inspired research enabled his countrymen to chart and conquer the mysteries of the vast oceans: in 1488 Bartolomeu Diaz rounded the Cape of Storms (Cape of Good Hope) at the southern tip of Africa; in 1498 Vasco da Gama reached Calcutta and so opened up the sea route to India; in 1500 Pedro Alvarez Cabral discovered Brazil, and the Portuguese became the first white men to reach, among others, China and Ethiopia and, in 1520, Magellan became the first to circumnavigate the globe. Portuguese supremacy held sway over the high seas and her empire spread over four continents. This control of sea trade was to become her chief source of wealth during the 15th and 16th centuries.

For sixty years, between 1580 and 1640, Portugal was united to Spain. The allegiance, however, proved disastrous for Portugal, who lost many of her overseas possessions, whilst being reluctantly included in Spain's quarrels with England, France and Holland. With growing resentment a group of Portuguese patriots expelled the Spanish in 1640, and placed on the throne the powerful Duke of Braganza, who took the title of John IV. Six years after his death his widow re-strengthened the Portuguese alliance with England by giving in marriage her daughter, Catherine, to Charles II.

In 1755 a terrible earthquake rocked the country and devastated a large part of Lisbon. It was largely due to the unremitting efforts of King José I's minister, Pombal, that the country was raised from its ashes.

After the Peninsular War of 1808-14, Napoleon's devastation left the country vulnerable to the destructive influences of internal strife, and the situation deteriorated as successive monarchies became more and more unpopular. In 1910, the Braganza dynasty was finally banished as the new régime proclaimed Portugal a republic.

During the First World War the country's military commitments to the English alliance resulted in grave social and economic loss, so neutrality became her policy during World War II. Dr. Salazar, professor of economics at Coimbra University, took control of the country's finances between 1928 and 1940 and successfully restored Portugal's financial credit. In various ministerial capacities, until incapacitated by a stroke in 1968, he was responsible for a great many reforms, including the Concordat with the Vatican, which clarified the position of the Catholic Church in Portugal.

Over the past decade liberalising measures have been introduced and, as modern technology continues to change the life-style in both town and countryside, Portugal's progress will enable her to take her place confidently in the European community.

Considered to be Portugal's most colourful province, Minho *right* and pictured *left* with the Serra do Gerês rising in the background, is noted for its carefully tended, rich green countryside, dominated by prolific vines. The lovely old town of Viana do Castelo *above*, lies at the mouth of the Lima River, whilst Ponte de Barca *above right,* its pretty houses clustered around the parish church, is typical of the picturesque towns of the region.

Shrouded in mist the mountains *below* rise above the sunset-flooded dam.

Standing on a densely wooded hill behind Braga, the church of Bom Jesus *right* is characteristic of Minho baroque architecture.

It was from the fortress castle of Guimarães *centre left* that Afonso Henriques declared Portugal a free and independent country in 1128.

Vila do Conde *below left* was a thriving ship building port during the years that witnessed the country's glory as a nation of great explorers and discoverers. Today the town is noted for its unique lace-making industry and its historical attractions include the huge convent of Santa Clara *above left*, with its beautiful tombs *above* and the medieval church *below*.

Over two-hundred years old, Portugal's most famous wine – Port – is grown exclusively in the Wine District of the Douro Valley in northern Portugal. Usually made from black grapes, the secret of this exquisite wine lies in the nature of the arid soil and hothouse temperature of the valley in which it is grown. Once the harvest is gathered the atmosphere about the vats is heady before the 'must' begins to ferment. After the 'must' leaves the presses it is loaded into great casks for transportation, to be matured by slow ageing in bottle or cask, such as the ones shown *above and right* in the renowned Cockburn Cellars, to a fullness ranging from sweet to semi-dry. Brandy, added during fermentation, 'fortifies' the wine and helps to preserve its natural sugar content. Port is divided into two great families, those of vintage and blended, and the vintage wines *above left*, taking upwards of twenty years to mature, must be decanted before drinking. The important oak casks are skilfully made in the Cooper's workshop *left*.

Overleaf is pictured the elegant tree-lined Avenida dos Aliados, in the prosperous port of Oporto.

Nestling on the banks of the Douro, Oporto *centre left and below left,* its wharves softly bathed by the setting sun *above left,* owes its livelihood to the mighty river. The bridge of Don Luis *above and overleaf* was the second to be constructed, in 1879, by an Eiffel-trained engineer, and with upper and lower roads took six years to finish.

Reminiscent of ancient Phoenician craft, the 'rabelos' *below and right,* transport, in time-honoured manner, the casks of wine between the harbours of Oporto and Vila Nova de Gaia.

In the Upper Douro Valley the steeply-
terraced vineyards slope down to the river
which meanders through the verdant
countryside past colour-washed wine
cottages *below* and sleepy villages *right*.

In Quinta da Foz *left* the grapes are ready
for harvesting and must be gathered with
infinite care, for only perfectly intact fruit
yields the precious Port wine. The
procession of 'borracheiros' *above*,
supported by long sticks, thread their way
down towards the wine presses, the heavy
baskets stoutly borne upon their backs.

Aveiro *right, above right and left,* its
streets crossing and re-crossing busy
canals like those of Holland, was once a
thriving seaport until a violent tempest, in
1575, was responsible for causing an
obstruction to the entrance of its port,
resulting in the formation of a long lagoon
or 'ria' which formed inside the barrier as
the waters stagnated. Stretching for miles,
the misty 'ria' remains and has become a
source of wealth as natives pole their
curved-prowed 'moliceiros' *above and
below* along the lagoon, combing its placid
waters for the iodine-rich seaweed to be
used as a powerful fertilizer.

Reputed to have one of the finest climates in Europe, Figueira da Foz *above and below right and above* is an Atlantic seaside resort situated at the mouth of the Mondego River.

Rising majestically above the ploughed rice fields of Montemor-o-Velho is the great ruined castle *left,* in the Mondego Valley.

Below can be seen a group of lobster fishermen carefully examining the day's catch.

The magnificent museum city of Coimbra *above*, built in tiers above the lazy Mondego River, was once Portugal's capital when held in fief from the king of Léon, by Count Henry of Burgundy. Of all its ancient buildings the superb University *below* ranks as supreme. Originally founded in Lisbon by King Dinis, in 1290, the University was re-established in Coimbra in 1540, and its most striking feature is considered to be the great baroque library *right*, donated by King João V, in 1716. Containing a million volumes, some of its finest are here shown resting upon gold-embossed shelves made of rare Brazilian woods. From the Machado de Castro Museum can be seen the University and the old Cathedral Dome *left*.

Grape-harvesting is shown *overleaf* in the carefully tended fertile valley.

Located about ten miles from modern Coimbra are the ruins of the old Roman town of Conimbriga *featured on these pages,* close to the village of Condeixa-a-Velha. One of the richest and most civilised cities of the Luso-Roman epoch, it was destroyed by the Swevian hordes in 458, in spite of the fortifications that were previously erected in an attempt to ward off the invading Goths and Visigoths who swept in from the east as the Romans withdrew their power.

For centuries the ruins lay covered, hidden under a layer of soil from which grew olive trees, until archeological diggings revealed magnificent columns, fountains, thermal baths, beautiful mosaics, and, a short distance away from the site, the ruins of an aqueduct.

The town-plan superbly illustrates the layout of a small Roman provincial settlement, and within the museum are documented not only the discoveries but also the impressions of the daily life within the community.

One of Portugal's most picturesque villages, Nazaré *overleaf,* is crammed every summer by tourists who fill the long sandy beach below the Pederneira cliff.

Stretching into the distance the lovely foam-fringed beach of Nazaré *left* belies the dangerous off-shore currents that make the important occupation of fishing particularly hazardous. For the Nazaré menfolk, however, danger is an accepted way of life, for the shifting ocean bed and tides make it impossible to build a stone jetty and the boats must be pushed into the waves from the sandy beach *overleaf*. Preparing tackle *above*, repairing fishing-nets *right* and travelling by donkey *below*, are all familiar scenes in this picturesque village.

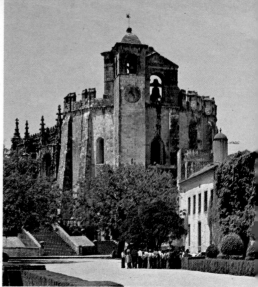

Throughout Portugal can be seen a rich storehouse of impressive monuments that bear witness to her glorious past. Old fortresses are set in exquisite, formal gardens *right;* magnificent monasteries, like those of Batalha *top left,* pale gold in the sunlight and begun in 1388 by the Dominican Order, and Tomar *above,* constructed by the Order of the Knights Templar on a wooded hill behind the town *below left* and which contains no fewer than seven cloisters, ranging in date from the 12th to the 17th century, dominate the landscape.

Religious shrines, such as the one to Our Lady of Fátima *below,* draw thousands in pilgrimages, and during the holy year of 1950 over a million pilgrims gathered on the vast esplanade to offer prayers for peace.

With tamarisk and periwinkles blooming at the foot of its high walls, Almourol *centre left* is a perfect example of a fairy-tale castle.

Glinting in the sunlight the lovely old town of Obidos *these pages* rises majestically above the Gaeiras vineyards off the main Oporto highway, and retains a graceful and dignified atmosphere within its unique 10th century Moorish fortifications. Passing through the town, the young bride of Dom Dinis was so captivated by 'the ramparts twining like a ribbon around a bouquet of shining white houses' that the king made her a present of Obidos, and from then on it became the wedding gift presented to the Queens of Portugal.

Sited on the famous Costa do Sol is one of Portugal's most sophisticated holiday centres, Estoril, pictured *overleaf*.

Rivalling Estoril in popularity is the elegant resort of Cascais featured on these pages, where the royal family and the court would come for part of the summer holidays. Still an important fishing village, the catches can be seen *right* as they are carried along the beach before being unloaded in the nearby, modern market. In the beautiful bay *top left* brightly painted boats bob in the blue water, and *above* is shown the busy Yacht Club Quay. From its vantage point on the rocky coastline the lighthouse *centre left* looks out towards the wild ocean. Beyond the red-tiled roofs can be seen Lisbon's magnificent Harbour *overleaf*.

Overlooking the Tagus River and backed by seven hills, Portugal's capital, Lisbon, is a charming blend of old and new. Lined on three sides by arcaded colonnades, the Praça do Comércio *above right*, known as Black Horse Square, is dominated by the magnificent equestrian statue of King Joseph I, whilst at the entrance to the ordered greenery of the Edward VII Park *below right* stands the imposing statue of the Marquês de Pombal, a minister under King Joseph, who was responsible for the rebuilding of the city after the disastrous earthquake of 1755. Palm trees and exotic flowers thrive in the Parque de Luis *above left; below left* is shown part of the reconstructed 12th century Romanesque Sé of Lisbon; *above* the Pantheon; *below* the memorial commemorating the Victory of Montes Claros in 1665 and *overleaf* the Basilica da Estrela overlooking the tawny "Sea of Straw".

Lisbon's oldest and most beautiful quarter is the Alfama *above,* its maze of narrow, twisting streets filled with the perfume of flowers and the lingering notes of the 'fado'. The Tower of Belém *centre right,* together with the exquisite Jerónimos (Heronymites) Monastery *below and right,* are particularly fine examples of Manueline architecture. Celebrating Portugal's immense achievements overseas is the impressive Monument of Discoveries *top right,* and *left* is shown the Avenida da Liberdade.

Solid walls *centre left* surround the ancient city of Evora, a Moorish town filled with a rich treasury of churches and museums that reveal its royal past. Directly opposite the Roman Temple of Diana *top left,* dating back to the 2nd century, stands the intriguing Pousada dos Lóios *above,* a luxury hotel installed in the former 16th century Convent of Los Lóios, whilst the Convent of Grace *bottom left,* founded in 1539 by John III, is just one of 31 monasteries and convents to be found in this fascinating capital of the Alentejo.

Sardines and swordfish are the main catch of the fishing fleet at Sesimbra *above right* whilst clay pots of all shapes and sizes *below* are offered for sale in the market at Setúbal.

Broad, sandy beaches with cliffs and strange rock formations *overleaf* are typical of the Algarve's unique beauty.

Lighthouses line the windswept Cabo de S. Vicente *centre left*, Europe's south-westerly extremity and regarded by the ancient mariners as the "World's End". Yet, whilst the Atlantic's breakers pound the rocky promontories, stretching along the Algarve coastline are wide, sandy beaches, little coves and placid lagoons *above left* that provide a perfect holiday playground *above and below*.

Praia da Rocha *below left and right* is a favourite all-year-round resort, having a mild climate, broad, golden sands, safe bathing and the intriguing caves and rocks that together form this holiday paradise. Even the Romans appreciated its charm, although they called it Abicada.

Retaining much of its original character in its steep, narrow streets, the delightful fishing village of Albufeira is one of the Algarve's most picturesque and popular resorts. Sun-bleached houses, hotels and Moorish churches cluster around Albufeira's unspoiled beach *overleaf*, which is connected to the village by an underground tunnel.

An international holiday centre, the Algarve's appeal lies in its many fine resorts that appear to be set in a garden overlooking the sea; Ferragudo *above left* is a small, picturesque village nestling on a peak above the Arade River; the tiny resort of Carvoeiro is shown *right*, a row of gaily painted boats lined up along its golden beach; *below right* is seen the charming village of Baleeira, its sandy cove washed by a tranquil ocean and the sweeping curve of Albufeira's superb beach is pictured *below*.

Once the Moorish Xelb, the lovely town of Silves *below left* is situated in the heart of the Algarve, its splendid 13th century castle still dominating the white-walled houses that cluster round its mighty walls.

Warm, summer sunshine, an azure sea
fringing soft, sandy beaches and a friendly
welcome all combine to make the Algarve
one of the most attractive holiday retreats.
For golf enthusiasts the course at Quinta
do Lago *bottom left* is ideal; sun
worshippers flock to Três Irmãos *centre
left*, the lovely Oceano Club *below* and
Club Praia da Oura *below right*, whilst
sailing is particularly popular at Vila
Moura *above right*. Clam fishers at Faro
are shown *top left* and pictured *overleaf* is
the tranquil valley and coastline of
Povoação in São Miguel, one of the
charming islands in the Azores that were
annexed by the Portuguese in the 15th
century.

First published in Great Britain 1979 by Colour Library International Ltd.
© Illustrations: Colour Library International (U.S.A.) Ltd, 163 East 64th Street, New York 10021.
Colour separated in Italy.
Display and text filmsetting by Focus Photoset, London, England.
Printed and bound by SAGDOS, Milan, Italy.
Published by Crescent Books, a division of Crown Publishers Inc.
Library of Congress Catalogue Card No. 79-84804
CRESCENT 1979